WELCOME TO MY COUNTRY

Welcome to
VENEZUELA

Gareth Stevens Publishing
A WORLD ALMANAC EDUCATION GROUP COMPANY

Written by
YUMI NG

Edited by
MELVIN NEO

Edited in USA by
JENETTE DONOVAN GUNTLY

Designed by
GEOSLYN LIM

Picture research by
SUSAN JANE MANUEL

First published in North America in 2005 by
Gareth Stevens Publishing
A World Almanac Education Group Company
330 West Olive Street, Suite 100
Milwaukee, Wisconsin 53212 USA

Please visit our web site at
www.garethstevens.com
For a free color catalog describing
Gareth Stevens Publishing's list of high-quality
books and multimedia programs,
call 1-800-542-2595 (USA) or
1-800-387-3178 (Canada).
Gareth Stevens Publishing's fax: (414) 332-3567.

© **MARSHALL CAVENDISH INTERNATIONAL (ASIA)
PRIVATE LIMITED 2004**
Originated and designed by
Times Editions Marshall Cavendish
A member of the Times Publishing Group
Times Centre, 1 New Industrial Road
Singapore 536196
http://www.timesone.com.sg/te

Library of Congress Cataloging-in-Publication Data
Ng, Yumi.
Welcome to Venezuela / Yumi Ng.
p. cm. — (Welcome to my country)
Includes bibliographical references and index.
ISBN 0-8368-3123-3 (lib. bdg.)
1. Venezuela — Juvenile literature. I. Title. II. Series.
F2308.5.N48   2004
987—dc22   2004041603

Printed in Singapore

1 2 3 4 5 6 7 8 9 08 07 06 05 04

PICTURE CREDITS
Agence France Presse: 3 (center), 14, 29, 37
A.N.A. Press Agency: 18, 25, 32
Art Directors and TRIP Photographic Library:
   3 (top and bottom), 4, 6, 7, 16, 27, 41
Jan Butchofsky/Houserstock, Inc.: 30
Chip and Rosa María de la Cueva Peterson:
   15 (top and bottom),17, 22 (top and
   bottom), 40
Victor Englebert: 24, 43, 45
Getty Images/Hulton Archive: 11, 39
John Gottberg/Houserstock, Inc.: 36
David Hoffman/Still Pictures: 35
Dave G. Houser/Houserstock, Inc.: 23, 28 (top)
The Hutchison Picture Library: cover, 5, 21,
   28 (bottom)
Lonely Planet Images: 9, 10 (top), 12, 13,
   33, 38
John Maier/Still Pictures: 26
Gil Moti/Still Pictures: 20
North Wind Picture Archives: 10 (bottom)
Heine Pedersen/Still Pictures: 34
Roland Seitre/Still Pictures: 1
David Simpson: 31
Travel Ink Photo and Feature Library: 2
Mireille Vautier: 19 (top and bottom)
Alan Watson/Still Pictures: 8

Digital Scanning by Superskill Graphics Pte Ltd

Contents

Words that appear in the glossary are printed in **boldface** type the first
time they occur in the text.

Welcome to Venezuela!

Venezuela's full name is the Bolivarian Republic of Venezuela. For over three hundred years, Venezuela was a **colony** of Spain. In 1823, the country won its independence. Today, Venezuela is one of the most modern nations in South America. Let's visit Venezuela and learn about its history and its people!

Opposite: A group of Venezuelans in Caracas cross a busy street. The city is home to over three million people.

Below: Many of the children living near the Orinoco Delta are very poor and live without even basic supplies.

The Flag of Venezuela

The flag of Venezuela has bands of yellow, blue, and red. The seven white stars stand for the seven **settlements** that united to fight against the Spanish in 1811. In the upper left-hand corner is the country's coat of arms.

The Land

Venezuela is the sixth-largest country in South America. It covers an area of 352,051 square miles (912,050 square kilometers). Land surrounds Venezuela to the west, south, and east. To the north is the Caribbean Sea. The Atlantic Ocean is to the northeast. Seventy-two Caribbean islands, including Margarita Island, are also part of Venezuela.

Left: A woman carries a load of wood through the Venezuelan Andes mountains in the state of Mérida.

Left: In the state of Amazonas, the Casiquiare River is an important source of water for the tropical rain forests. The Casiquiare River joins the Orinoco River, which is the country's longest and largest river.

Venezuela has three main regions: the Cordillera, the Llanos, and the Guiana Highlands. The Cordillera region has many mountains, which are part of the Andes mountain chain. Bolívar Peak, the highest point in the country, is located in the Cordillera region. The peak is 16,428 feet (5,007 meters) high. The Llanos, or Plains, region is a huge, flat area of grassland that covers about one-third of Venezuela. The Guiana Highlands region covers almost half of the country. It is full of a thick growth of **tropical** plants and trees.

Climate

Venezuela has two seasons. The wet season is from May to October, and the dry season is from December to March. The average temperature in Venezuela is 82° Fahrenheit (28° Celsius). High in the mountains, above about 6,500 feet (2,000 m), average temperatures fall below 75° F (24° C). Above 9,800 feet (3,000 m) snow often covers the land.

Left: Venezuela is near the **equator**, so it has a tropical climate all year. Most of the plants and trees in the country, including rain forests such as this one, stay green. Forests cover about 30 to 40 percent of the entire country. Tall grasses cover about 50 percent of the land.

Plants and Animals

Many Venezuelan plants are tropical. Others, such as orchids and tree ferns, are **subtropical**. High in the mountains, only lichen and alpine shrubs can grow. Venezuela has many animals, such as deer, bears, monkeys, jaguars, and pumas. In the forests, poisonous coral snakes and rattlesnakes live alongside nonpoisonous boa constrictors and massive anacondas. More than 1,300 types of birds also live in Venezuela, including tanagers, storks, and parrots.

History

People lived in Venezuela as long ago as the Stone Age. They settled in the country around 10,000 B.C. and most likely came to the country from Asia. Over thousands of years, the first Venezuelan Indians were replaced by the Arawaks, Caribs, and Chibchas. The Arawaks were peaceful Indians who built large villages along the coast.

Above: Most Venezuelan Indians do not follow a traditional way of life. Instead, most of them wear modern clothes and speak Spanish. The Waraos and the Yanomamis are two of the largest Indian groups left in Venezuela that have kept their cultures and customs alive.

Left: This drawing shows one Indian man making his way through the thick undergrowth of a lush rain forest as other men swim in a nearby river.

Left: This picture shows Christopher Columbus on one of his ships. The famous explorer was Italian, but he worked for the Spanish. In 1498, Columbus became the first known European to reach what we know as Venezuela. He laid claim to the land for Spain.

The Caribs were very aggressive, and most of them settled on the islands off the coast of Venezuela. The Chibchas were the most advanced of these groups and settled in the valleys of the Andes.

The First Europeans Arrive

In 1498, Venezuela was claimed by the Spanish. At first, the Spanish were not interested in forming colonies. Instead, they allowed traders from England and France to look for pearls and gold. By the late 1500s, however, the Spanish had begun to take an interest and had built many colonies in Venezuela.

Colonial Life

As the Venezuelan colonies grew, so did the need for workers. The Spanish began to take Indians as slaves and forced them to dive for pearls and mine gold. They were also forced to care for fields of sugarcane, tobacco, and cacao, the beans used to make chocolate. Many Indians died in **rebellions** against the Spanish, but an even larger number died from diseases carried to Venezuela from Europe. By 1740, Venezuelan **exports** were bringing in lots of money.

Left: Jajo is a small mountain town in the state of Trujillo. It was founded by the Spanish in 1611. Through the years, Jajo's old colonial buildings and roads have been carefully maintained.

Left: At one time, Simón Bolívar's family owned this sugarcane farm in the state of Aragua. During the fight for independence, the freedom fighter used the farm as a base for soldiers. Simón Bolívar is now regarded as a national hero and is considered the founding father of Venezuela.

Most of the money from Venezuelan exports went to the Spanish. Spaniards also held all top government positions in the colonies. The **Creoles**, who lived in the Venezuelan colonies, grew angry and began to protest. In 1810, a group of Creoles **overthrew** Venezuela's top Spanish officials. On July 5, 1811, the Creoles, led by famous freedom fighter Simón Bolívar and General Francisco de Miranda, declared the independence of the colonies. The Spanish soon took back the country, however. Venezuela became truly independent in 1823.

Left: Since 1998, Hugo Chávez Frías has been president of Venezuela. In 2002, the military tried to take power away from him, but they did not succeed.

Troubled Leadership

From 1830 to 1935, a series of harsh military leaders headed Venezuela's government. The leaders often fought other political groups in the country for power. The fighting led to a civil war from 1859 to 1863. The country was a **democracy** from 1945 to 1948. By 1951, Venezuela had again been taken over by harsh leaders. Oil prices rose during the 1970s. Venezuela's economy improved for a short time. Since the late 1970s, increasing poverty has led to more power struggles.

José Antonio Páez (1790–1873)

General José Páez helped Venezuela gain its independence. Páez became president in 1831 and governed the country for eighteen years. Although he was harsh, his laws brought peace and economic progress to Venezuela.

José Antonio Páez

Rómulo Gallegos Freire (1884–1969)

Before becoming president in 1947, Rómulo Gallegos Freire was a writer. His most famous novel was *Doña Bárbara* (1929). As president, he helped build industries and improved health care, housing, and education.

Irene Sáez Conde (1961–)

In 1981, Irene Sáez Conde won the Miss Universe beauty pageant. She later got a degree in political science. From 1992 to 1998, as mayor of a part of Caracas, she helped improve public services. From 1999 to 2000, she was governor of the state of Nueva Esparta.

Rómulo Gallegos Freire

Government and the Economy

The government of Venezuela has three branches: executive, legislative, and judicial. The president of Venezuela is the head of the executive branch and of the armed forces. Each president serves a six-year term and is elected by voters. The president chooses members of the Council of Ministers, who serve as advisers. The government's legislative branch consists of a congress, which is called the National Assembly. Its 165 members are elected by voters.

Left:
All meetings of the National Assembly take place in the National Capitol. The building is in Caracas, the capital city of Venezuela.

The Supreme Tribunal of Justice heads Venezuela's judicial branch. The tribunal is the country's highest court of law. It oversees Venezuela's system of lower courts.

Venezuela is divided into twenty-five governmental regions, and each has its own elected governor. Of the regions, twenty-three are states. One is a federal district and includes the capital city of Caracas. The last region is a group of seventy-two islands in the Caribbean Sea.

Above:
The government office for the state of Zulia is in the city of Maracaibo.

The Economy

Most of Venezuela's economy is based on its oil industry. To keep the country from relying too much on oil for its income, President Hugo Chávez made economic rules designed to help other industries develop. Instead of helping, Chávez's rules hurt the economy. In 2002, Venezuela's economy crashed. Before the crash, over 50 percent of Venezuelans lived in poverty. Today, the number is probably even higher.

Left: Oil rigs off the coast of Venezuela pump oil from the ocean floor. Since the 1920s, almost all of Venezuela's income has been made from selling oil and oil products.

Left: Venezuela's Llanos region, in the center of the country, is good for raising cattle.

Farming and Industries

Venezuela produces many food crops, including bananas, coffee, corn, rice, and sugarcane. Farmers also raise cattle on the country's plains, and fishermen catch fish and shellfish near the coast.

Making **petrochemicals** and refining oil are important Venezuelan industries. Other industries include making home appliances, leather, paper, and fabrics. Venezuela also has mines and factories that produce metals such as iron.

Below: Aluminum is one important Venezuelan export. Other important exports include iron, steel, fruits and vegetables, and goods such as television sets and radios.

People and Lifestyle

About 67 percent of Venezuelans are *mestizos* (mays-TEE-sohs), or people with a mix of European and Indian or African **ancestors**. Most of their European ancestors were Spanish, but some were Italian, Portuguese, or German. Today, about 10 percent of the people are African Venezuelans. Less than 2 percent of the population are purely Indian.

Below:
In Venezuela, there are slightly more men than women. The population is also very young. Over half of all Venezuelans are under twenty-five years old.

The Upper and Lower Classes

When the Spanish ruled Venezuela, the people were divided into two different classes. People in the upper class were called "decent people," and they were all European. People in the lower class were called "common people." They were mestizo, Indian, or African Venezuelans. In Venezuela today, class is determined by how much money a person has, not by his or her race. Rich people now form the upper class, and poor people form the lower class.

Above: Only rich Venezuelans can afford to live in these houses. The gap between how the rich and poor live in Venezuela is getting wider. The rich live very well, but more than half of all Venezuelans are now poor and do not have enough food or access to proper health care and education.

Family Ties

Venezuelans are very close to their families. Many grandparents, parents, and children live together. The whole family, including uncles and aunts, often helps raise the children. Many parents follow the Roman Catholic tradition of choosing godparents for their children. The godparents are most often close friends of the family. They play an important role in the child's religious education.

Above:
For over twenty years, women in Venezuela have pushed to get the same opportunities as men. Having an education makes it possible for these women to get good jobs and to hold important positions in society.

Left: In the past, Venezuelan women stayed at home and took care of the children. Today, however, many Venezuelan women work outside of the home.

City and Country Life

Today, most Venezuelan people live in cities. Venezuela's largest cities are Caracas, Maracaibo, Valencia, and Barquisimeto. From the 1940s to the 1970s, many Venezuelans living in the countryside moved to the cities to work for the oil industry. The population of the cities grew quickly, and there were not enough houses for everyone. The government tried to build more houses, but many people ended up living in **shantytowns** on the edges of the city.

Above:
Shantytowns are called *ranchos* (RAHN-chohs) in Venezuela. The first ranchos did not have electricity, sewer systems, or water. Some of the ranchos, such as these in Caracas, now have basic services, and many are being changed into permanent housing structures.

Education

Venezuela's education system consists of three levels: elementary school, secondary school, and higher education. Elementary school lasts for nine years and provides a basic education. There are two types of high schools in the country. One type lasts three years and provides **vocational** courses. The other type of high school lasts two years and prepares students for college.

Below:
This schoolteacher in Venezuela is training students to think creatively. She uses the methods created by Dr. Edward de Bono (1933–).

Higher Education

Venezuela has about thirty colleges and universities. University programs, such as engineering or medicine, last four to six years. The country also has more than one hundred other institutes of higher learning, which usually offer programs in subjects such as foreign languages or technology, including computer programming. The programs last from two and half to three years.

Above:
This painting of Ernesto Guevara (1928–1967) covers the outer wall of the Central University of Venezuela in Caracas. Guevara was a well-known **revolutionary.** The words to the left of the painting are part of a speech given by Guevara. In it, he says that all people should be able to get an education, not just those in the upper class.

Religion

About 96 percent of Venezuelans are Roman Catholic, but not all of them practice their religion regularly. Since the 1980s, many people have left the Catholic religion to join the **Protestant** religion, which includes the Baptist and Lutheran branches. Protestantism is Venezuela's fastest-growing religion. It has grown about four times larger in the country since 1981.

Left: Venezuelan **Muslims** worship at the Al Ibrahim Mosque in Caracas, which was built in 1994. A mosque is a house of worship for people who practice the religion of Islam. The Al Ibrahim Mosque is the only mosque in Venezuela.

Other Beliefs

A small number of Muslims and Jews are present in Venezuela. The country has fifteen **synagogues** for Jewish worshipers. Some Venezuelans also belong to African and Indian religions.

Language

Spanish and Other Languages

The official language of Venezuela is Spanish. Spanish colonists brought the language to the country in the sixteenth century. There are also more than thirty Indian languages in Venezuela. Most of the Indians speak Spanish and their own languages. In far-off regions, they do not speak Spanish at all. Today, many Venezuelans speak English as a second language. Small groups of Venezuelans also speak Arabic, Chinese, or German.

Above:
A man in Caracas reads a newspaper report about Hugo Chávez and his win in the presidential election of 1998.

Left: Newsstands in Caracas sell many different magazines and newspapers. Most Venezuelan magazines and newspapers are written in Spanish.

Left: Arturo Uslar Pietri (1906–2001) is one of the most popular authors in Venezuela. In 1991, he won the Rómulo Gallegos Prize for Literature for his novel *Una visita en el tiempo*, or *A Visit in Time*.

Literature

During the Spanish colonial years, the literature written in Venezuela was mostly **chronicles** and poems. In the 1800s, the battle for independence led many Venezuelan authors to write passionate books. The literature of Francisco de Miranda, Simón Bolívar, and Andrés Bello became famous and their works influenced authors such as Manuel Romero García (1861–1917), who wrote *Peonia* (1890). Today, the country's literature is a unique mix of styles from Venezuela's **ethnic** groups.

Arts

Painting and Sculpture

Many Venezuelan artists use European, Indian, Caribbean, and African styles in creating works of art, theater, music, and dance. Before the Spanish arrived, Venezuelan Indians created lots of rock carvings, cave paintings, and pottery. After the Spanish arrived, the Catholic Church influenced the country's art. Most artworks created were religious.

Below:
The Plaza Bolívar is the subject of this artist's painting. The plaza, or town square, is regarded as the heart of colonial Caracas.

Following Venezuela's battle for independence, many artists began to use the country's struggles in their art. One Venezuelan artist, Martín Továr y Továr (1827–1902), painted a famous **mural** in which Simón Bolívar wins a great victory against the Spanish.

Besides paintings and sculptures, Venezuelan artists also create many crafts, including musical instruments, saddles, ropes, high-quality pottery, hammocks, and canoes.

Above: Venezuelan artist Jesús Soto (1923–) is famous for his kinetic art, such as this piece. The art hangs in front of a building in Caracas. Kinetic art gives the viewer the impression of movement.

Music

Venezuelan music is very lively. It combines Spanish, African, and Indian rhythms and sounds. The northeastern coast of Venezuela is famous for its African beats. To the west, in the state of Zulia, gaita is a traditional style of music. Gaita musicians make up new, rhyming songs as they play a small guitar and *maracas* (ma-RAH-cas).

Below: This man makes musical instruments in his shop. He is holding a *cuatro* (coo-AH-troh), a small, four-stringed guitar used to play gaita.

Architecture

Good examples of Spanish colonial architecture, including government buildings, churches, and homes, still stand in the old sections of Caracas and other cities. Some of Venezuela's most impressive buildings are modern. The University City of the University of Caracas includes a concert hall, a sports complex, and many other magnificent buildings. Construction began in 1944 and took sixteen years.

Above: Many of Venezuela's old colonial houses, such as these houses in central Maracaibo, have been carefully repaired and painted in many bright colors.

Leisure

Most Venezuelans like to spend their free time with their families. Often, they go out to restaurants with their friends and families rather than eat at home. Many Venezuelans also enjoy going to the movies, although most of the movies are from foreign countries and have Spanish **subtitles**. Going to theater performances is another popular leisure activity.

Below: Bullfights are popular events in Venezuela. They are held most often during holidays and festivals. The sport was brought to the country from Spain.

Dancing is a very important part of Venezuelan culture. Many Venezuelans dance at parties or festivals or go out to nightclubs. A lot of Venezuelans like to visit the many art museums and art galleries found in Caracas.

Venezuelans also spend leisure time outdoors enjoying the many kinds of landscapes in the country. Canoeing, visiting caves, and bird-watching are favorite pastimes. Many people swim or fish at the country's beaches, too.

Above:
Many tourists in Venezuela take nature-viewing trips by canoe. These tourists are seeing the sights along a branch of the Orinoco River.

Left:
Many Venezuelans enjoy water sports, such as swimming, windsurfing, water skiing, diving, and snorkeling, along the country's long coastline.

Sports

Venezuelans enjoy many sports, from martial arts to rugby and basketball. Many Venezuelans also enjoy hiking, rock climbing, mountain biking, hang gliding, and horseback riding in nature reserves and national parks. The game *bolas criollas* (BOH-lahs cree-OH-yahs), or lawn bowling, is also popular. The object is to roll a wooden disc next to a small ball without touching it.

Venezuela's most popular sport is baseball. The sport became popular in the early 1900s when North Americans moved to Venezuela to work in the oil industry. They brought the game with them. By the mid-1900s, Venezuela had a professional baseball league. The country now has a winter league, which begins in October. The winning team represents Venezuela in the Caribbean Series, a regional competition.

Below: A player from Venezuela's team, Magallanes Navegantes (*left*), slides onto second base as a player from the Dominican Republic's team, Tigres de Licey, tries to tag him. The two teams were competing in the 2002 Caribbean Series, which was held in Caracas.

Religious Festivals

Most Venezuelans are Roman Catholic, so many of the country's festivals are religious. Some festivals are celebrated nationwide, including Holy Week and the Cross of May. Holy Week ends on Easter Sunday and celebrates the days before Christ's death. During the Cross of May, people decorate large wooden crosses with flowers and sing and pray to the Holy Cross. Regional festivals also are held in honor of **patron saints**.

Below: During the Catholic festival of Corpus Christi, men dress like devils in masks and bright red costumes. They dance through the streets making lots of noise and stop only when they come to a church. At the church, the "dancing devils" pretend to be afraid. The festival honors the belief that evil can never win out over good.

National Holidays and Festivals

Venezuela's national holidays include Independence Day on July 5 and Simón Bolívar's birthday on July 24. Día de la Raza, or Day of the Race, is on October 12. It celebrates the Spanish traditions of **Latin Americans**.

Carnival is one of Venezuela's most celebrated events. The festival is held on the Tuesday before Ash Wednesday. Dancing, brightly colored floats, and noisy parades are all part of Carnival.

Above: Carnival takes place in either February or March. During Carnival, people dress in colorful clothes and masks. They often dance to lively music and watch parades throughout the day.

Food

Venezuela's most popular food is the *arepa* (ah-REH-pah). Arepas are cakes made of corn flour, water, and salt. They can be eaten plain or with fillings. For breakfast, arepas are often filled with *perico* (peh-REE-koh), a mixture of onions, tomatoes, and scrambled eggs. At lunch, people enjoy arepas stuffed with salad, cheese, or meats, including beef and sausage.

Below: This woman is tapping a grilled arepa to check if it is done. Arepas are very popular and usually take the place of bread in Venezuelan meals.

The national dish of Venezuela is *Pabellón Criollo* (pah-beh-YOHN cree-OH-yoh), which is a stew made from shredded beef. It is usually eaten with black beans, fried **plantains**, and rice. *Hallaca* (ah-YAH-kah) is a dish traditionally served at Christmas. The mixture includes cornmeal, vegetables, meats, and herbs wrapped in plantain leaves. Many kinds of tropical fruits, including mangoes and coconuts, grow in Venezuela and are very popular.

Above: Sidewalk cafés, like this one in the Sabana Grande district of Caracas, are popular. The cafés serve Venezuelan coffee, which is famous for its mild and delicate taste.

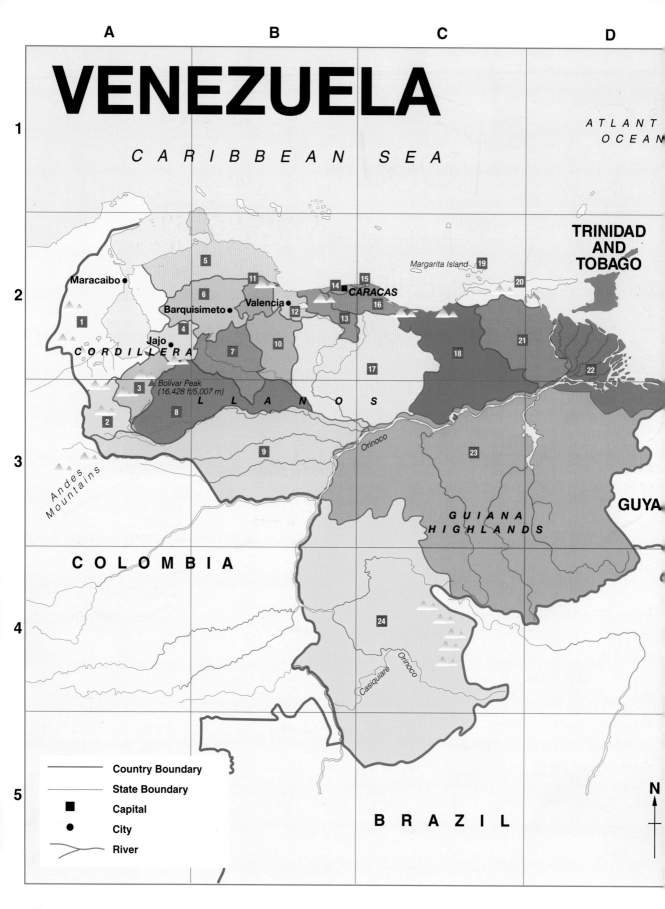

VENEZUELA

A   *B*   *C*   *D*

C A R I B B E A N   S E A

ATLANT OCEAN

TRINIDAD AND TOBAGO

Margarita Island   19

Maracaibo ●

5

11

6

15

14 ■ **CARACAS**

20

Barquisimeto ●   Valencia ●

12

16

C O R D I L L E R A

Jajo ●

1

4

7

10

13

18

21

17

3   ▲ Bolívar Peak
(16,428 ft/5,007 m)

22

2

8

L   *L*   *A*   *N*   *O*   *S*

9

Orinoco

23

GUYA

Andes Mountains

*G U I A N A
H I G H L A N D S*

COLOMBIA

24

Orinoco

Casiquiare

	Country Boundary
	State Boundary
■	Capital
●	City
	River

N

B R A Z I L

42

Above: Many species of birds live in the tropical rain forests of Venezuela.

Andes
   Mountains A3
Atlantic Ocean D1

Barquisimeto B2
Bolívar Peak A3
Brazil B4–D5

Caracas B2
Caribbean Sea
   A1–C2
Casiquiare River
   B4–C4
Colombia A1–B5
Cordillera (region)
   A2–A3

Guiana Highlands
   (region) C3–D4
Guyana D3–D4

Jajo A2

Llanos (region)
   B3–C3

Maracaibo A2
Margarita Island C2

Orinoco Delta
   D2–D3
Orinoco River
   B3–D2

Orinoco River
   (odd branch)
   B3–C4

Trinidad and
   Tobago D2

Valencia B2

States

1 Zulia
2 Táchira
3 Mérida
4 Trujillo
5 Falcón
6 Lara
7 Portuguesa
8 Barinas
9 Apure
10 Cojedes
11 Yaracuy
12 Carabobo
13 Aragua
14 Distrito Federal
15 Vargas
16 Miranda
17 Guárico
18 Anzoátegui
19 Nueva Esparta
20 Sucre
21 Monagas
22 Delta Amacuro
23 Bolívar
24 Amazonas

Quick Facts

Official Name   The Bolivarian Republic of Venezuela

Capital   Caracas

Official Language   Spanish

Population   25,700,000 (2003 estimate)

Land Area   352,051 square miles (912,050 square km)

Regions   Amazonas, Anzoátegui, Apure, Aragua, Barinas, Bolívar, Carabobo, Cojedes, Delta Amacuro, Distrito Federal, Falcón, Guárico, Lara, Mérida, Miranda, Monagas, Nueva Esparta, Portuguesa, Sucre, Táchira, Trujillo, Vargas, Yaracuy, Zulia.

Major Cities   Caracas, Barquisimeto, Maracaibo, Valencia

Highest Point   Bolívar Peak 16,428 feet (5,007 meters)

Major River   Orinoco River 1,590 miles (2,560 km)

Main Religion   Roman Catholicism

Religious Festivals   Corpus Christi, Cross of May, Holy Week

National Holidays and Festivals   Carnival, Day of the Race, Independence Day, Simón Bolívar's birthday

Currency   bolívar (VEB 1,600.00 = U.S. $1 as of 2004)

Opposite: Fish such as the sharp-toothed piranha can be found in the rivers of Venezuela.

Glossary

ancestors: family members from the past, farther back than grandparents.

chronicles: descriptions of events in history written in date order.

colony: a settlement in one country that is controlled by another country.

Creoles: people born in Spanish colonies who had purely Spanish ancestors.

democracy: a government in which citizens elect their leaders by vote.

equator: an imaginary line that divides the Earth into two equal halves.

ethnic: related to a group of people who have similar customs and languages.

exports (n): products sent out of a country to be sold in another country.

Latin Americans: people who live in the Americas south of the U.S. and who have Spanish ancestors.

maracas: instruments that are made from gourds and that are used as rattles.

mural: a large picture painted directly onto a wall or ceiling.

Muslims: people who belong to the religion of Islam.

overthrew: removed from office or brought down or defeated.

patron saints: saints who are believed to protect places or groups of people.

petrochemicals: chemicals taken from oil or natural gas.

plantains: a fruit similar to a banana.

Protestant: relating to a branch of the Christian religion that separated from the Catholic religion in the 1500s.

rebellions: fights against a government or a ruler.

revolutionary: a person who believes in ideas that are new and very different.

settlements: small communities set up by people from other lands or areas.

shantytowns: poor towns made up of shacks or temporary homes.

subtitles: the movie's words translated and shown below the movie picture.

subtropical: relating to areas that border tropical regions but are not quite as hot or as damp as tropical climates.

synagogues: houses of worship for people who follow the Jewish religion.

tropical: relating to very warm and wet regions where plants grow all year.

vocational: related to an occupation, profession, or skilled trade.

More Books to Read

Amazon Diary: The Jungle Adventures of Alex Winters. Hudson Talbott (Putnam Publishing Group)

The Amazonian Indians. Anna Lewington (Peter Bedrick Books)

Baseball in the Barrios. Henry Horenstein (Gulliver Books)

Monkeys of Central and South America. True Book series. Patricia A. Fink Martin (Children's Press)

The Orinoco River. Carol B. Rawlins (Franklin Watts, Inc)

Rainforest Colors. Science Emergent Readers series. Susan Canizares and Betsey Chessen (Scholastic)

Venezuela. Countries, Faces, and Places series. Patrick Merrick (Child's World)

Venezuela. Enchantment of the World series. Terri Willis (Children's Press)

Venezuela. A Ticket to series. Helga Jones (Carolrhoda Books)

Videos

Amazon: Land of the Flooded Forest. (National Geographic)

Animals of the Rainforest. (Schlessinger Media)

Plants of the Rainforest. (Schlessinger Media)

Venezuela. South America series. (Ernst Interactive Media)

Web Sites

cyberschoolbus.un.org/infonation/ index.asp

en.wikipedia.org/wiki/Venezuela

www.atozkidsstuff.com/ven.html

www.embavenez-us.org/kids.venezuela/ intro.htm

Due to the dynamic nature of the Internet, some web sites stay current longer than others. To find additional web sites, use a reliable search engine with one or more of the following keywords to help you locate information about Venezuela. Keywords: *Bolivar Peak, capybara, Hugo Chavez, Jesus Soto, Margarita Island, Simon Bolivar, Warao.*

Index